I0558092

Focus to Fortune

Profitable Time Management for Busy Minds

Cindy Baker

CBC – Cindy Baker Coaching Press

ISBN: 979-8-9927781-0-6

Book production by MysticqueRose Publishing Services LLC

To my husband, Richard. I could not
have had such success without
your love and support.

Thank you for believing in me.

I love you very much.

Contents

What Others Are Saying About Cindy:

CINDY AS A SPEAKER:

"Cindy speaks to the struggle many of us face in managing so much information, so many tasks, so many daily pressures. She offers small, actionable steps that really help! My daily tasks are now *rocks, pebbles, and sand* and I am getting much more done! Her warmth and humor are so engaging, it was a pleasure to hear her speak!"

—*Leslie Gordon, Ph.D.,*
Speech & Accents Expert, TEDx Coach, National Speakers Association President

"Cindy Baker is a powerhouse of energy and positivity! She electrifies the room, transforming procrastination into productivity and distractions into dollars. Her dynamic insights on focus and leveraging ADHD for entrepreneurial success make her a must-have speaker for any stage looking to inspire massive action and unstoppable momentum!"

—*Kim Walsh Phillips,*
Keynote Speaker, Founder of Elite Speakers Network

CINDY AS A COACH:

"The program was a game changer for me. The support I received from Cindy and the other group members helped me know I am not alone and gave me ideas that I hadn't considered on my own. Each lesson inspired me and broke down things into achievable steps and accountability without pressure.... It gave me new ideas to manage my time better and be more organized. Overall, as a result of joining the program, I feel more confident in myself as a person with ADHD."

—*Liesl D.,*
LPC-MHSP, Behavioral Health

"I was tired of the cycle of setting out with big plans to do so much and then having to start over at the drawing board again! Cindy really understands ADHD in a practical way. She knows what tools it takes to turn weak areas into strengths. This has changed my whole life from managing time to resolving conflict in relationships. Cindy is relatable, accessible, compassionate and has the knowledge that works for adults with ADHD."

—*Holly K., Entrepreneur*

"I was really struggling to complete anything and needed to figure out how to change it. I decided I needed help to make this change and took a chance signing up for Cindy Baker's program after watching her free seminar. I felt the program would help give me tools and accountability to make changes necessary. It has helped give me a roadmap to get me on track and more organized to be able to prioritize tasks and help me get them done. It is still a work in progress but it is helping me stay on track. I am glad I took a leap of faith and joined the program."

—*Doug S., Entrepreneur*

"I feel like the program has helped me to make some changes I was looking for, but I know it is an ongoing growth process as well. … I have learned a lot…I have made small changes, mostly in how I see myself and little habits each day. The biggest thing is I don't feel so down on myself."

—*Marion K., Entrepreneur*

"The weekly group calls were enjoyable and I met some pretty terrific people. I have become much kinder to myself and embrace my superpowers that I have when I'm hyper focused. I still have Cindy's voice inside my head when I get overwhelmed. She is such a kind, understanding and knowledgeable teacher, I wish I knew her when I was in school. Cindy is so relatable, I have never met someone that understood how my mind works! She's a blessing."

—*Cathy M., Fashion Industry Logistics Manager*

Preface

UNDERSTANDING THE BUSY MIND AND TIME MANAGEMENT CHALLENGES

"Busy." That was always my answer when people would ask me how I was doing. I said it secretly hoping for sympathy. I wore my busyness as a badge of honor, as if being busy somehow made me more valuable. But underneath all the constant activity was something else— frustration.

I felt like the proverbial hamster on the wheel, wearing myself out with constant running but never getting anywhere. Through my late-in-life diagnosis of ADHD, my master's in counseling, and my research and practice of productivity strategies, I eventually learned that wishing for more hours in the day was not the answer. Trying to get more done just left me overwhelmed and exhausted.

The feeling of never being or doing enough made me feel like a failure. What I eventually learned, and what this book is about, is that having more time isn't the answer. Creating the life we want is about how we choose to spend the time we already have. Sometimes productivity is about doing less, not more.

If you are a busy professional, maybe you can relate. Meet Alex, a talented entrepreneur with a wealth of creative ideas and a bustling business. Alex can think outside the box, connect ideas that seem worlds apart, and generate innovative solutions on the spot. But there's one thing Alex constantly struggles with: managing time.

Each day starts with enthusiasm and a long list of tasks that need attention. But somewhere between a morning brainstorming session and the first sip of coffee, Alex's focus scatters. A quick check of emails turns into a two-hour dive into unexpected projects. That critical task he planned to tackle by noon? It's now lost in the shuffle of fifteen browser tabs, a dozen half-started emails, and a flurry of notifications. By the end of the day, Alex is mentally exhausted, having worked hard but feeling that very little got done.

Sound familiar? Many entrepreneurs—especially those with ADHD like me—face this challenge. Creative minds like Alex's excel at generating ideas and thriving in dynamic environments, but they often struggle to harness their energy and focus it in a productive way.

The good news? You don't have to change who you are to make time work for you. With the right strategies, you can create systems that turn your unique thinking style into a superpower, allowing you to accomplish more while reducing stress and driving profitability. This book is designed specifically for entrepreneurs like Alex—and like you—who want to manage time in a way that supports your goals and maximizes your business success.

WHY PROFITABLE TIME MANAGEMENT MATTERS

Time management isn't just about checking off tasks or squeezing more into your day. For entrepreneurs, especially those with busy minds, it's about strategically allocating time to the tasks that drive profits. Mastering time management doesn't just help you get more done; it directly impacts your bottom line.

Entrepreneurs with ADHD or high-energy, creative minds often face a unique set of challenges in traditional time management systems. Concepts like rigid schedules, endless to-do lists, or strict time-blocking can feel restrictive, even impossible to maintain consistently. But by adapting strategies that fit your brain's natural wiring, you can build a sustainable approach to time management that allows you to thrive.

Here's what effective, ADHD-friendly time management can do for you:

- **Increase Productivity:**
  By reducing distractions and focusing on high-impact tasks, you'll accomplish more in less time.

- **Reduce "Overwhelm":**
  With a clear plan, there's less scrambling to figure out what's next, freeing up mental energy.

- **Drive Profitability:**
  When you're consistently working on the right tasks, the ones that lead to growth and revenue, your business will benefit from more predictable, steady profits.

In essence, profitable time management is about channeling your focus where it counts. This book is designed to help you overcome the obstacles that come with a busy mind and harness that energy to make a real difference in your business.

WHY TRADITIONAL TIME MANAGEMENT FAILS BUSY MINDS

Traditional approaches to time management often assume a linear, orderly way of thinking that doesn't align well with the creative mind. For entrepreneurs with ADHD traits, focus comes in bursts, motivation can be fleeting, and even the most detailed plans can go off track. When these approaches fail, it's easy to feel like managing time is an impossible task. But the problem isn't with you—it's with the methods that don't consider your unique strengths.

What if, instead of forcing yourself into rigid systems, you could use methods that work with your brain? This book will guide you through strategies like working with your energy cycles, breaking tasks into manageable sprints, and creating ADHD-friendly routines that fit seamlessly into your life. By applying techniques tailored to busy minds, you'll not only get more done, but you'll also see an improvement in your productivity, confidence, and profitability.

THE STRUCTURE OF THIS BOOK

Each chapter in this book is packed with practical tips, real-life examples, and actionable exercises designed to help you implement what you've learned.

Here's what you can expect:

- **Strategies for assessing where your time goes** and how to identify which tasks drive profit and which ones drain your time and energy
- **Techniques for structuring your day** in a way that works with your natural rhythms so you can maximize focus during high-energy periods
- **Tools for managing distractions** and staying on track, even in a world full of constant interruptions
- **Methods for setting boundaries and saying "no"** to low-value activities, allowing you to spend time on high-impact tasks
- **Systems for building sustainable routines** that support your long-term success

HOW TO USE THIS BOOK

The methods in this book are designed to be adaptable. Try them, adjust them, and make them work for you. Busy minds thrive on flexibility, and no two days may look exactly alike. But by following these strategies, you'll build a stronger foundation for profitable time management, even on days when focus feels elusive.

At the end of each chapter, you'll find practical exercises to help you put each concept into action. Whether you're just starting your business or running an established company, this book will give you the tools to make time work in your favor and turn focus into fortune.

Time management is really the management of your focus. In this book, you will discover how to utilize this formula for maximizing your focus:

F.O.C.U.S.

F – Filter Your Priorities
Identify what truly matters in your business and life. Focus on the tasks and goals that align with your values and drive the greatest impact. Eliminate or delegate the rest.

O – Organize Your Time and Space
Set up your environment and schedule to minimize distractions and maximize productivity. Use tools, systems, and techniques to streamline your workflow and create structure.

C – Commit to Consistent Action
Break your goals into smaller, manageable steps, and take intentional action every day. Consistency over time leads to meaningful results, even if progress feels slow at first.

U – Utilize Your Strengths
Leverage your unique abilities, whether it's creative problem-solving, hyperfocus, or adaptability. Play to your strengths instead of trying to fit into a productivity mold that doesn't suit you.

S – Set Boundaries to Protect Your Time
Say no to distractions, interruptions, and tasks that don't align with your priorities. Create clear boundaries around your time and energy to stay on track and prevent burnout.

CHAPTER 1

Assessing Your Time Landscape

AUDIT YOUR TIME: WHERE IS IT GOING?

"You may delay, but time will not."

— Benjamin Franklin

One of the most crucial steps to mastering time management is understanding how you currently spend your time. If you've ever felt like your day has disappeared in a blur of tasks without significant progress, you're not alone. Many entrepreneurs, especially those with ADHD or scattered focus, find themselves busy but not productive.

To make impactful changes, you need to start with a clear picture of where your time is actually going. This process is called a time audit. It may sound tedious, but it's the foundation for improving your time management skills and ultimately driving more profits in your business.

Time Blindness

People with creative brains have a different awareness of time than others. And this creates unique problems for them—especially with all of the distractions we face in today's digital society. Adults with ADHD like me often have struggles with organization and time management because inconsistency and forgetfulness get in the way.

These time management struggles are not character flaws. They stem from the unique way our brains are wired. Entrepreneurial brains tend to be reactive. They respond to whatever comes into their immediate vicinity—making it harder to stay focused and on track with projects, especially if the work is boring, repetitive, or overly complicated.

If a big project feels overwhelming, it is tempting to "microfocus" and get lost in a small detail in order to block out the "overwhelm." We need to clean the entire kitchen, for example, so we charge in there with all of our cleaning supplies, determined to tackle the task. Two hours later, we are on the floor scrubbing the grout between the tiles with a toothbrush and the kitchen is still a mess. We feel busy, but we are not moving any closer to our goals.

And we often underestimate the amount of time a task will require (by a lot). This leads us to feel rushed and behind, doing things at the last minute and staying stressed and exhausted. This is why a time audit can be so useful.

Poor awareness of time is a very common trait. You are not alone! For the person with a distracted mind, everything tends to run together in their brains. They often do not see natural breaks such as hours or minutes. If you experience the passing of time as a constant, unpredictable flow, it may be extremely difficult for you to accurately gauge the passage of time. This is why I encourage my coaching clients to use an analog clock or kitchen timer so they can actually see how much time has passed and how much is left.

STEVE JOBS

Steve Jobs, the legendary cofounder of Apple, was known for his relentless focus on high-impact tasks. He has a quote that states, "Your time is limited, so don't waste it living someone else's life." Early in his career, he realized that he was spending too much time on minor issues, like handling administrative tasks or responding to endless emails. He felt like it was important to identify where he was wasting time and use his time wisely.

Jobs began delegating low-impact tasks to his team, freeing himself to focus on product development and strategic thinking. This shift allowed him to pour his energy into designing revolutionary products like the iPhone, which not only transformed the tech industry but also boosted Apple's profits exponentially. If he was still staring at the computer and could not solve a problem after ten minutes, he would get up and take a walk. The lesson here is clear: understanding where your time goes is the first step to reclaiming it for higher-value activities.

HOW TO CONDUCT YOUR OWN TIME AUDIT

You don't have to be a tech visionary like Steve Jobs to benefit from examining how you spend your time. Here's a simple, ADHD-friendly approach to get started:

1. **Choose Your Tracking Method:**
   You can use a physical notebook, a time-tracking app like **Toggl**, or a spreadsheet. Pick a method that feels natural and easy for you. Write down ordinary tasks that you typically do each day like getting ready, cleaning up the dishes, commuting to work, checking emails, and the like. Then write your estimate of how long that task usually takes to complete.

2. **Track Everything for a Week:**
   Record each task you do throughout the day, noting the actual start and stop times. Don't judge or edit yourself—just observe. The goal is to collect data without worrying about how it looks.

3. **Analyze the Data:**
   At the end of the week, review your entries. How accurate were your estimates? Highlight tasks that directly contribute to your business's profits. These might include activities like client meetings, marketing campaigns, or product development. Next, look for patterns of time-wasting activities like excessive social media use or constant email checking.

4. **Identify Time-Wasters and Profit-Boosters:**
   Create two lists: one for time-wasting activities and one for high-impact, profit-boosting tasks. This will help you see where you need to make adjustments.

By conducting a time audit, you'll have a clear picture of your current time usage. This is the first step toward redirecting your energy into tasks that grow your business and increase profitability.

SPOTTING HIGH-IMPACT TASKS (HITS)

"Things which matter most must never be at the mercy of things which matter least."

—Johann Wolfgang von Goethe

Once you have a clear view of your time landscape, the next step is identifying the tasks that have the highest impact on your business. These are your High-Impact Tasks (HITs). They're the activities that drive growth, boost profits, and align with your business goals. In contrast, low-impact tasks might keep you busy, but they don't move the needle.

For example, it may feel productive to spend an hour on Canva trying to get the perfect color scheme or graphic for a social media post, but is that really going to make you more money? No. Not directly, anyway. We will discuss perfectionism later, but a good goal is to learn to be OK with completing something on time that is only 95–98% perfect. My coaching clients know that two of my favorite mantras are "Done beats perfect" and "Progress over perfection."

RICHARD BRANSON AND HIS HITS

Richard Branson, the founder of the Virgin Group, attributes much of his success to focusing on HITs. He is known for asking himself, "Will this activity move the business forward, or is it a distraction?"

In the early days of Virgin Records, Branson had a habit of micromanaging small, day-to-day tasks. He soon realized that this approach was not sustainable if he wanted to grow the business. Instead, he began to focus on larger, strategic initiatives—like signing major artists—that would have a significant impact on the company's profitability. He also prioritizes physical health and fitness. He has said that exercise doubles his productivity. By prioritizing HITs, Branson was able to build a global brand that encompasses music, airlines, and even space travel.

HOW TO IDENTIFY YOUR HITS

Here's how you can identify the High-Impact Tasks in your own business:

1. **List Out Your Regular Tasks:**
   Write down all the tasks you perform in a typical week. Include everything, from checking emails and social media to meeting with clients and working on projects.

2. **Evaluate Each Task's Impact on Profit:**
   Ask yourself: Does this task directly contribute to my revenue or business growth? If the answer is yes, it's likely a HIT. For example, writing a proposal for a potential client is a HIT, while spending an hour on Instagram may not be.

3. **Prioritize HITs in Your Schedule:**
   Once you've identified your HITs, make sure they are prioritized in your daily schedule. These tasks should be the focus of your peak productivity times, when your energy and focus are at their highest.

By focusing on HITs, you can make better use of your time and ensure that you are spending your energy on activities that truly drive your business forward.

THOMAS EDISON: FOCUS ON THE MOST VALUABLE USE OF TIME

Thomas Edison, one of history's greatest inventors, was known for his relentless work ethic. He often worked up to twenty hours a day, driven by his passion for innovation. However, Edison understood that simply working long hours was not enough. He needed to focus his time on tasks that would lead to meaningful discoveries and profit.

Edison famously said, "Genius is 1 percent inspiration and 99 percent perspiration." But he didn't mean that all effort was equal. He prioritized experimentation and problem-solving over administrative tasks. For instance, while inventing the electric light bulb, Edison and his team tested thousands of materials to find the right filament. Instead of giving up when a test failed, Edison viewed each failure as valuable feedback, focusing his time on learning from mistakes and trying new approaches.

Just like Edison, by focusing on high-impact activities and using each failure as a stepping stone, entrepreneurs can maximize the value of their time and make breakthroughs that lead to significant business growth.

AVOIDING COMMON PITFALLS

"Quality is never an accident; it is always the result of high intention, sincere effort, intelligent direction and skillful execution; it represents the wise choice of many alternatives."

— William A. Foster

While conducting a time audit and identifying HITs, it's important to be mindful of common pitfalls that can derail your efforts:

1. **Getting Stuck in Analysis Paralysis:**
   It's easy to get bogged down in analyzing your time without taking action. Remember, the goal is to identify patterns and make adjustments, not to overthink every detail.

2. **Overloading Your Schedule with HITs:**
   While it's tempting to pack your day with as many HITs as possible, this can lead to burnout. Instead, aim to complete 2–3 high-impact tasks per day. This manageable approach helps maintain focus without overwhelming your mind.

3. **Neglecting Breaks and Downtime:**
   For busy minds, taking breaks might feel counterproductive, but it's essential. Short, intentional breaks help you recharge and maintain productivity throughout the day. Use the Pomodoro Technique, through which you work in 25-minute bursts with 5-minute breaks, or try 90-minute focus sprints with longer breaks in between.

PRACTICAL EXERCISE: THE TIME AUDIT CHALLENGE

To put these concepts into action, try the following exercise:

1. **Choose a Week for Your Audit:**
   Pick a week where you can commit to tracking your time every day. Use a simple tool, like a notebook or an app, and log every activity you perform.

2. **Analyze and Reflect:**
   At the end of the week, review your logs. Identify patterns, highlight time-wasters, and pinpoint HITs.

3. **Make One Change:**
   Choose one time-wasting habit to eliminate and one HIT to prioritize more consistently. Notice the difference in your productivity and sense of accomplishment.

INSPIRATION TO TAKE ACTION

"If you always do what you've always done, you'll always get what you've always got."

—Henry Ford

Understanding where your time goes is the first step toward reclaiming it. By conducting a time audit and focusing on HITs, you are laying the foundation for more effective and profitable time management. Small changes, repeated consistently, can lead to significant results.

In the next chapter, we'll dive into how to structure your day to maximize these High-Impact Tasks, setting you up for consistent progress and profit.

CHAPTER 2

Designing a Time-Optimized Workday

FINDING YOUR PRODUCTIVITY PEAKS: LEVERAGING ENERGY CYCLES

"The most efficient way to live reasonably is every morning to make a plan of one's day and every night to examine the results obtained."

— Alexis Carrel

Every entrepreneur has moments throughout the day when they feel their energy soar and times when they feel drained. Understanding these natural rhythms, often referred to as **ultradian cycles**, can help you design a workday that aligns with your peak productivity periods.

WINSTON CHURCHILL: A MASTER OF ENERGY MANAGEMENT

Winston Churchill, the British prime minister during World War II, was a master of energy management. Despite the intense pressure of his role, he was known for maintaining a consistent daily schedule that optimized his energy.

Churchill woke up early, but instead of immediately diving into work, he spent the first few hours of his day reading newspapers, writing, and having a light breakfast— all while still in bed. By midmorning, he felt recharged and ready to handle meetings and strategic planning. In the afternoon, he would take a nap, a practice he believed was crucial for maintaining his stamina throughout the day. This brief rest allowed him to extend his working hours late into the night, making critical decisions that shaped the course of history.

Churchill's schedule wasn't conventional, but it worked for him. By aligning his activities with his natural energy cycles, he managed to stay productive and effective, even during the most stressful times.

Understanding your energy peaks and designing a schedule that takes advantage of them can significantly boost your productivity. You don't have to follow a traditional 9-to-5 routine; instead, find what works best for you and stick to it.

THE POWER OF THE 90-MINUTE FOCUS SPRINT

"The key to success is to focus our conscious mind on things we desire, not things we fear."
– Brian Tracy

One of the most effective time management techniques for busy minds is the **90-minute focus sprint**. This method is based on research that shows our brains work best in bursts of focused activity, typically lasting around 90 minutes, followed by a short rest period. This cycle mirrors our natural ultradian rhythms, where periods of high mental activity are followed by dips in energy.

SERENA WILLIAMS: TRAINING IN FOCUSED SPRINTS

Serena Williams, one of the greatest tennis players of all time, uses a similar concept in her training regimen. Her practice sessions are structured into focused, intense bursts of activity, followed by short breaks. During these sprints, she gives 100% effort, honing her skills and pushing her limits.

This approach helps her maintain peak performance during matches, as she's trained her mind and body to work at maximum capacity for short periods. By mimicking this pattern in her matches, she can maintain focus and stamina, even under immense pressure.

Applying the concept of focused sprints to your work can help you maximize productivity. By working intensely for 90 minutes and then taking a 10–15-minute break, you allow your brain to recharge, making it easier to maintain focus throughout the day.

How to Implement 90-Minute Focus Sprints:

1. **Identify Your Task:**
   Choose a high-impact task you want to focus on during your sprint.

2. **Set a Timer:**
   Use a timer to set a 90-minute window for uninterrupted work. Eliminate distractions and commit to focusing solely on the task.

3. **Take a Break:**
   Once the timer goes off, take a 10–15-minute break. Use this time to stretch, walk around, or grab a healthy snack to recharge.

MORNING ROUTINES: SETTING THE TONE FOR SUCCESS

*"Your morning routine generates a 10x
return for good or for bad. Make it strong!"*

— Tim Ferriss

A well-designed morning routine can set the tone for a productive day. For busy entrepreneurs, especially those with ADHD, a structured morning routine can help clear mental clutter, establish focus, and kickstart momentum. The key is to create a routine that energizes you and prepares your mind for the tasks ahead.

My day starts with coffee and reading, journaling, and praying. After looking at my calendar and planning my day, I take the dogs on a short walk, have breakfast, and then work on deep-focus activities for one hour to one and a half hours. Then I break and go to a midmorning exercise class at the gym. This is what works for me.

THE STORY OF HOWARD SCHULTZ: A MORNING RITUAL FOR FOCUS

When I was a single teacher, I found myself short about $400 every month, so I decided to get a second job as a barista at a new Starbucks coffee shop opening near me. I figured it would be a fun part-time job and might even allow me a chance to meet "Mr. Right." I was surprised at how well-organized the franchise is.

Howard Schultz, former CEO of Starbucks, attributes much of his success to his disciplined morning routine. Schultz wakes up at 4:30 a.m. and starts his day with a workout. He believes that physical exercise helps him clear his mind and set a positive tone for the day. After his workout, Schultz spends time with his family, enjoying a cup of coffee and discussing the day ahead. This ritual allows him to feel connected and grounded before diving into the demands of running a global coffee empire.

By the time he arrives at the office, Schultz is fully awake, focused, and ready to tackle the day's challenges. His morning routine provides a sense of stability and sets a strong foundation for his productivity.

Establishing a morning routine that includes activities like exercise, journaling, prayer, or planning can help busy entrepreneurs start the day with clarity and purpose. It doesn't have to be long or complicated; even a 30-minute routine can make a significant difference.

Tips for Creating an Effective Morning Routine:

1. **Start with a Calming Activity:**
    Whether it's meditation, journaling, or a simple breathing exercise, start your day with a calming activity to center your mind.

2. **Incorporate Movement:**
    Physical activity, even if it's just a quick stretch or walk, can help wake up your body and boost your energy levels.

3. **Plan Your Day:**
    Take a few minutes to review your tasks and set priorities. Identify your top 2–3 HITs (High-Impact Tasks) for the day.

BATCHING TASKS:
THE SECRET TO REDUCING DECISION FATIGUE

"It's not the daily increase but daily decrease.
Hack away at the unessential."

— *Bruce Lee*

Task batching is a powerful strategy that involves grouping similar tasks together to complete them in one focused session. This technique helps reduce the time lost to context-switching (the mental effort of shifting from one task to another) and minimizes decision fatigue, a common issue for entrepreneurs juggling multiple responsibilities.

THE STORY OF TIM COOK: BATCHING EMAILS FOR EFFICIENCY

Apple CEO Tim Cook is known for his intense work ethic and efficient time management. One of his strategies is batching his emails. Instead of responding to emails throughout the day, Cook dedicates specific times to tackle his inbox. By batching this task, he reduces the mental load of constantly switching between emails and other work, allowing him to focus better on strategic decision-making.

Cook's approach is simple yet effective. By minimizing interruptions and focusing on similar tasks in one go, he maintains his productivity and keeps his attention on the company's most pressing issues.

Takeaway: Batching tasks like responding to emails, making phone calls, running errands, or even scheduling social media posts can help you streamline your work and stay focused on more critical activities.

How to Start Task Batching:

1. **Identify Routine Tasks:**
   List out tasks you do frequently, such as answering emails, social media updates, or content creation.

2. **Group Similar Tasks Together:**
   Schedule time blocks to handle these tasks in batches instead of spreading them throughout the day.

3. **Stick to Your Schedule:**
   Resist the urge to check emails or social media outside your designated time block.

THE IMPORTANCE OF BUFFER TIME: PLANNING FOR THE UNEXPECTED

"If you want more time, freedom, and energy, start saying no."

— Anonymous

No matter how well you plan, unexpected interruptions and urgent tasks will inevitably pop up. This is where **buffer time** comes in. Buffer time is a period set aside in your schedule to handle unplanned events or to catch up on tasks that took longer than expected. It acts as a safety net, preventing your entire day from being derailed by unexpected disruptions. Just like this book has margins so that the words do not spill off the edge of the page, we need margins in our day.

So many unexpected things can happen, and if there is no margin in your schedule, those things can throw your whole day off. My dad used to always say that a project always cost more and takes longer than you think it will so plan accordingly. Even if you are an awesome planner, thinking that you have plenty of time and not accounting for the unexpected is a recipe for disaster.

JEFF BEZOS: THE POWER OF FLEXIBILITY

Jeff Bezos, the founder of Amazon, is known for his strategic thinking and time management. Bezos intentionally leaves "white space" in his calendar, allowing for flexibility and the opportunity to tackle unexpected issues that arise. This buffer time helps him stay responsive and make quick decisions without feeling overwhelmed by a packed schedule.

Bezos's approach emphasizes the importance of not overloading your calendar. By leaving room for unexpected tasks, he maintains a clear mind and the ability to focus on high-impact decisions that drive Amazon's growth.

Takeaway: Incorporate buffer time into your daily schedule to handle unexpected interruptions. This practice can reduce stress and help you maintain control over your day, even when surprises arise.

ACTION STEPS TO DESIGN YOUR IDEAL WORKDAY

To help you implement these concepts, try these practical steps:

1. **Identify Your Peak Productivity Times:**
   Pay attention to when you feel most focused and energized. Use this time for your most important tasks.

2. **Create a Daily Schedule:**
   Design a daily routine that includes morning rituals, 90-minute focus sprints, and buffer time.

3. **Test and Adjust:**
   Experiment with different schedules and routines. Track your productivity and adjust as needed until you find what works best for you.

By designing a time-optimized workday that leverages your natural energy cycles and minimizes distractions, you set yourself up for consistent, profitable progress.

STARTING NOW

"Don't wait. The time will never be just right."

— Napoleon Hill

Remember, your time is your most valuable asset. By designing a workday that maximizes your productivity, you're investing in both your business and your personal growth. Start now, even if your system isn't perfect—because progress is always better than perfection.

START SMALL, AIM BIG

It's easy to get overwhelmed when trying to overhaul how you manage your time. The key is to start small. Focus on one or two strategies from this chapter that resonate with you, and gradually add more as you build confidence. The momentum you create will inspire you to refine and improve your approach over time.

For example: Consider the story of James Clear, author of *Atomic Habits*. He didn't overhaul his life overnight; instead, he focused on making small, 1% improvements every day. Over time, these small, consistent changes compounded into massive transformations in his productivity and success.

VISUALIZE YOUR IDEAL DAY

One powerful exercise is to visualize your perfect workday. Picture yourself starting the day with clarity, working on meaningful tasks without interruptions, and ending the day feeling accomplished and in control. Use this visualization as your guide to creating the systems and routines that will get you closer to this ideal day.

Practical Tip: Write down your vision of an ideal workday and identify one actionable step you can take today to move closer to it.

Accountability and Support

Sometimes, the best way to stick to your time management goals is to involve others. Share your intentions with a trusted colleague, mentor, or coach who can hold you accountable.

Richard Branson, the founder of Virgin Group, emphasizes the importance of surrounding yourself with the right people. He credits much of his productivity to the team and advisors who help him stay focused on his goals.

FINAL THOUGHT: TAKE THE FIRST STEP

As the saying goes, "A journey of a thousand miles begins with a single step." Taking control of your time is a journey. The sooner you begin, the sooner you'll start seeing results—not just in your business, but in your sense of fulfillment and peace of mind.

Your first step may be as simple as setting a timer for 25 minutes and focusing on one task, or as big as redesigning your workspace to eliminate distractions. Whatever it is, take it today. Your future self—and your business—will thank you.

CHAPTER 3

Managing Distractions and Staying on Track

INTRODUCTION: THE CONSTANT BATTLE WITH DISTRACTIONS

"You will never reach your destination if you stop and throw stones at every dog that barks."

— Winston Churchill

In today's fast-paced digital world, distractions are one of the biggest hurdles to effective time management, especially for entrepreneurs with ADHD. Whether it's a notification on your phone, a knock at your door, or a wandering mind, distractions can derail your focus and consume valuable time. We get easily sidetracked when there is an interruption.

I remember it was a Tuesday afternoon, and I was in the middle of my usual "scroll break." You know, just a few minutes to check my phone...which turned into thirty minutes of watching puppy yoga on YouTube. Don't judge —it was very inspiring. Downward dog, anyone?

The problem was, I had a big deadline looming. And instead of tackling it, I was stuck in what I like to call the "procrastination spiral." You know the one: "I'll start after I check my email." Then suddenly you're researching the history of bubble wrap. And you say to yourself, "While I'm here, let me just reorganize my desktop icons...because obviously, that's urgent." By the time you come up for air, you've accomplished nothing except learning that bubble wrap was originally designed as wallpaper.

Time slips away so easily when we're distracted. But here's what I realized that day: I wasn't just procrastinating. I was giving away my *dreams*, minute by minute, in tiny, unplanned breaks. All the time I spent on distractions was time I wasn't spending building the life and business I wanted. Procrastination wasn't just stealing my time—it was stealing my future. And that hit me hard—right after puppy yoga ended, of course. Maybe you can relate.

In this chapter, we'll explore strategies for managing both external and internal distractions to help you stay on track and maintain momentum in your business.

ELIMINATING EXTERNAL DISTRACTIONS

The first step in managing distractions is to control your environment. External distractions are often easier to tackle because they come from sources outside of yourself. By making intentional adjustments to your workspace and using certain tools, you can create a distraction-free environment that supports focus and productivity.

ADHD-FRIENDLY TECHNIQUES FOR SETTING UP A DISTRACTION-FREE WORKSPACE

A well-organized and intentional workspace can be a game-changer for entrepreneurs prone to distractions.

Here are some proven techniques:

1. **Designate a Focus Zone:**
   Create a specific area for deep work that is free from clutter and interruptions. This space should be reserved for your most important tasks, signaling to your brain that it's time to focus when you're there.

2. **Minimize Visual Clutter:**
   Keep only essential items on your desk. Visual clutter can be overwhelming and distracting, especially for those with ADHD. Try using trays, boxes, or desk organizers to keep your workspace tidy.

3. **Use Noise-Canceling Headphones:**
   If you're easily distracted by sounds, consider using noise-canceling headphones or listening to white noise, instrumental music, or focus-enhancing soundtracks.

4. **Strategic Use of Lighting:**
   Natural light is best for maintaining energy and focus. If natural light isn't an option, opt for bright, warm lighting that reduces eye strain and keeps you alert.

TOOLS AND STRATEGIES FOR MINIMIZING NOTIFICATIONS AND INTERRUPTIONS

"The difference between successful people and really successful people is that really successful people say no to almost everything."

— Warren Buffett

Notifications are a common source of distraction, pulling your attention away from your work.

Here's how to handle them:

1. **Digital Detox Hours:**
   Schedule specific times in your day to disconnect from your phone, emails, and social media. For example, use tools like **"Do Not Disturb" mode** on your phone during deep work sessions.

2. **Notification Management:**
   Go through your apps and disable unnecessary notifications. Prioritize which alerts are genuinely important and silence the rest.

3. **Time-Blocking Apps:**
   Use time management apps like **Freedom** or **StayFocused** to block distracting websites and limit social media usage during work hours.

4. **Set Boundaries with Others:**
   Inform colleagues, family members, or roommates about your focus times. Set clear boundaries to minimize interruptions. For example, use a "Do Not Disturb" sign or signal when you're in deep work mode.

OVERCOMING INTERNAL DISTRACTIONS

While external distractions are easier to control with environmental changes, internal distractions require self-regulation and mental strategies. Internal distractions, such as impulsive thoughts or daydreaming, can be especially challenging for those with ADHD.

Adults with ADHD, like me, find it difficult to block out distractions and often forget to return to the previous task they were engaged in after a distraction has occurred. When our brains bounce randomly from one focus to the next, we easily lose track of time. The key is to develop techniques to recognize when your mind is wandering and refocus quickly.

This reminds me of what I like to call "The Internet Rabbit Hole." Let's say I was doing research for this book. So, I start searching for something on the Internet. Then you know what happens next. I happen to see a headline for a news story. It is an attention-grabbing headline, and I start scanning to satisfy my curiosity. But then something in the story reminds me of a friend. And then I remember, "I never responded to her email!" So, I immediately switch over to email. I scan the list, and several have such compelling subject lines that scream out "Aren't you curious? Read me now!" I then find myself reading emails. One requires an immediate response, so I start typing. Just then my phone dings with a text message notification, and before you know it, I have spent thirty minutes on my phone watching puppy yoga videos again!

Another source of internal distractions is the barrage of thoughts in our head that we battle when trying to be productive—those sneaky, self-sabotaging thoughts that derail our focus.

These are things like:

- "I'm not good enough to do this."
- "This will never be perfect, so why bother?"
- "I should be working on something else."
- "I'll never catch up, so I might as well not even start."

Here's the thing: Most of the time, our external distractions (phones, emails, people interrupting) aren't the real problem. **The real productivity killer is happening in your mind.** But the good news? We can take back control.

First, let's understand why this happens. Your brain LOVES certainty. It wants to keep you safe and comfortable. So, when you sit down to do something important, your brain throws doubt at you because it's trying to protect you from failure, embarrassment, or wasted effort.

But the problem is that this "protection" actually **keeps you stuck.** It keeps you from finishing that project, writing that email, launching that idea, or making money in your business.

STRATEGIES FOR CURBING IMPULSIVE THOUGHTS

So, what do we do? We can't just tell our brain to "shut up." (If only it were that easy!) Instead, we have to **retrain our thoughts.** And I'm going to give you three powerful strategies to do just that.

1. Interrupt & Replace:

For example:

You sit down to work and your brain says "This is too hard. I can't do this."

STOP. Instead of accepting that thought as truth, interrupt it.

Replace it with something empowering:

- Instead of "I can't do this," say "This is new, but I can figure it out."
- Instead of "I'm too far behind," say "I'm taking action, and that's what matters."
- Instead of "It has to be perfect," say "Done is better than perfect."

What's one self-sabotaging thought you catch yourself thinking?

2. The 5-Minute Proof Experiment:

This is perfect for when your brain tells you "I can't do this," "I'm not motivated," or "This will take forever."

Instead of arguing with that thought, prove your brain wrong—in just five minutes.

Here is how it works:

1. Set a 5-minute timer.
2. Start working, even if you feel resistance.
3. At the end of five minutes, ask, "Was my brain right? Was this impossible?"

Ninety-nine percent of the time, you'll find that once you start, you keep going.

3. Talk to Your Future Self:

This is for when your brain says "I'll just do it later."

Instead of listening to "present you" (who wants to procrastinate), ask: **What would "future me" want?**

Future you would LOVE to have this done.

Future you would rather relax knowing the work is finished.

Future you doesn't want to deal with the stress of last-minute chaos.

When you connect with your future self, **you make better choices now.**

Additional Strategies:

1. **Mindfulness Practice:**
   Mindfulness helps increase awareness of your thoughts and improves your ability to refocus. Even a simple 5-minute breathing exercise before starting a task can center your mind and reduce impulsivity.

2. **The 2-Minute Rule:**
   If a distracting thought or task comes up and it can be done in under two minutes, take care of it quickly or jot it down to handle later. This way, the thought is acknowledged but doesn't pull you completely off track.

3. **Task Batching for Impulsivity:**
   Group similar small tasks (like checking emails or returning calls) and tackle them at set times. This reduces the frequency of task-switching and helps contain impulsive urges to check messages throughout the day.

TECHNIQUES FOR RECENTERING ON TASKS

"Focus is a matter of deciding what things you're not going to do."

— John Carmack

1. **Self-Check-Ins:**
   Set a timer for every 30 to 60 minutes to pause and check in with yourself. Ask, "Am I on task? What was I originally trying to accomplish?" This habit can help you catch yourself if you've been unintentionally sidetracked.

2. **Visualization:**
   Before starting a task, take a moment to visualize yourself completing it successfully. This can enhance your focus and help you stay committed to the task.

3. **Setting Mini Goals:**
   Breaking down tasks into smaller, manageable goals can help maintain your focus. For example, instead of tackling a large project all at once, set a goal like "I will write 200 words in the next 20 minutes." This creates a clear, achievable target and reduces the likelihood of distraction.

USING TIME ANCHORS TO STAY ON TRACK

A time anchor is a preplanned checkpoint during your day that helps you stay on track with your schedule. These can be as simple as scheduled breaks, meetings, or self-check-ins.

THOMAS EDISON: ANCHORING FOCUS THROUGH ROUTINES

As mentioned earlier, Thomas Edison was known for his incredible focus and productivity. He famously used specific time anchors throughout his day, such as breaks and scheduled naps, to recharge and refocus. Edison would work intensely for hours but used short, planned naps as a way to reset his mind, allowing him to return to his work with fresh energy and focus.

Takeaway: Time anchors are a way of structuring your day around specific points of reference. By having these anchors, you create a framework that helps guide you back to your tasks even when distractions occur.

PRACTICAL EXERCISES TO BUILD FOCUS

1. **Daily Distraction Log:**
   Keep a small notepad by your workspace. Every time you get distracted, jot down what it was. After a week, review the log to identify common distractions and brainstorm strategies to eliminate or minimize them.

2. **The Pomodoro Technique:**
   Use this time management method, which involves working in 25-minute focused intervals followed by a 5-minute break. This rhythm helps train your mind to focus and reduces the likelihood of succumbing to distractions.

3. **Environmental Tweaks:**
   Experiment with small changes to your environment each week, such as adjusting your desk position, lighting, or background sounds. Keep a record of how these changes impact your focus.

CONCLUSION: THE POWER OF MASTERING DISTRACTIONS

"You can't do big things if you're distracted by small things."

—Unknown

Managing distractions is not about eliminating them entirely; it's about recognizing them quickly and using effective strategies to return to your task. By taking control of both external and internal distractions, you create an environment and mindset that allows you to stay on track and make significant progress toward your goals.

CHAPTER 3

Mastering the Art of Prioritization

INTRODUCTION: THE POWER OF PRIORITIZATION

*"The key is not to prioritize what's on
your schedule but to schedule your priorities."*

— Stephen Covey

When you have a million things on your to-do list, how do you decide where to start? For entrepreneurs with busy minds, everything can feel equally urgent, making it hard to determine which tasks will actually move the needle. This is where prioritization comes in. It's about distinguishing between what's important and what's merely urgent, allowing you to focus on high-impact tasks that drive growth and profits.

In this chapter, we'll explore practical methods to prioritize your tasks, the common pitfalls of prioritization, and techniques to align your daily actions with your long-term goals.

THE PARETO PRINCIPLE: FOCUSING ON THE VITAL FEW

*"It's not enough to be busy, so are the ants.
The question is: What are we busy about?"*

— Henry David Thoreau

One of the biggest challenges entrepreneurs face is deciding what to focus on first. With endless to-do lists, emails, meetings, and tasks vying for our attention, it's easy to get lost in the busyness of work without making meaningful progress. The key to cutting through the noise is mastering the art of prioritization.

The **Pareto Principle**, also known as the 80/20 rule, is a powerful tool for prioritization. It states that roughly 80% of the results come from 20% of the efforts. In other words, a small fraction of your tasks will yield the most significant impact on your business.

How to Apply the 80/20 Rule:

1. **Identify High-Impact Tasks:**
   Analyze your to-do list and pinpoint which tasks are likely to have the biggest impact on your business goals. These are your "vital few" tasks.

2. **Eliminate or Delegate Low-Impact Tasks:**
   Recognize the tasks that take up a lot of time but yield minimal results. Delegate them, automate them, or eliminate them if possible.

3. **Focus on the 20%:**
   Dedicate your most productive time to working on these high-impact tasks. This ensures that your energy is spent on activities that generate the most value.

CASE STUDY: APPLE AND THE 80/20 RULE

Steve Jobs famously used the 80/20 rule when he returned to Apple in 1997 and realized the company was struggling. He noticed that Apple was working on too many projects, spreading its resources thin.

One of his first actions was to drastically simplify Apple's product line. He famously took a marker to a whiteboard and drew a two-by-two grid, indicating only four products: a consumer desktop, a pro desktop, a consumer laptop, and a pro laptop. Jobs then eliminated all other products from Apple's lineup.

Jobs cut down the product line by 70%, focusing on the few core products that were driving the majority of revenue. By narrowing the focus of the entire company to just four products, Jobs ensured that every effort was directed toward excellence in these areas. This ruthless prioritization helped Apple turn around and become one of the most valuable companies in the world.

Takeaway: Like Jobs, entrepreneurs must learn to say no to good opportunities to focus on the great ones. Identifying your HITs requires evaluating your tasks and choosing the ones that will make the most significant impact.

IDENTIFYING YOUR HITS: HIGH-IMPACT TASKS

*"If you have more than three priorities,
you don't have any."*

— Jim Collins

How to Identify Your HITs:

1. **List All Tasks:**
   Write down all the tasks you need to accomplish.

2. **Assess Impact vs. Effort:**
   Rate each task based on its potential impact and the effort required.

3. **Choose Your Top 3 HITs:**
   Select the three tasks with the highest impact and focus on completing them first.

By applying the 80/20 rule, you can concentrate on the most impactful tasks, leading to significant improvements in productivity and profitability. If you are a business owner, the majority of your time should be spent on revenue-producing activities.

THE STORY OF WARREN BUFFETT: THE 2-LIST STRATEGY

Warren Buffett, one of the world's most successful investors, uses a simple yet effective method for prioritization, known as the **2-List Strategy**. The story goes that Buffett once asked his personal pilot to write down his top twenty-five career goals. After the pilot listed them, Buffett asked him to circle the top five.

Buffett then asked the pilot what he planned to do with the remaining twenty goals. The pilot responded that he would work on them intermittently. Buffett corrected him: "No. Everything you didn't circle just became your 'avoid at all cost' list. These items get no attention from you until you've succeeded with your top five."

Takeaway: The 2-List Strategy emphasizes the importance of ruthless prioritization. It's not enough to know what's important; you must also be clear about what is *not* a priority. This approach forces you to focus on the few tasks that will drive the most results.

THE EISENHOWER MATRIX: A TOOL FOR DECISIVE ACTION

"What is important is seldom urgent,
and what is urgent is seldom important."

— Dwight D. Eisenhower

The **Eisenhower Matrix**, developed by former U.S. President Dwight D. Eisenhower, is a prioritization tool that helps you decide on and prioritize tasks by urgency and importance.

It divides tasks into four categories:

1. **Urgent and Important:**
   Tasks you must do immediately (e.g., handling a critical client issue)

2. **Important but Not Urgent:**
   Tasks you should schedule for later (e.g., strategic planning, professional development)

3. **Urgent but Not Important:**
   Tasks you can delegate (e.g., responding to non-critical emails)

4. **Not Urgent and Not Important:**
   Tasks you should eliminate (e.g., excessive social media scrolling)

THE STORY OF DWIGHT EISENHOWER: STRATEGIC DECISION-MAKING

Eisenhower's ability to manage his time and priorities was instrumental in his leadership during World War II. As Supreme Commander of the Allied Expeditionary Force, he faced numerous urgent and critical decisions daily. He often said, "The urgent are not important, and the important are never urgent."

This mindset helped him delegate urgent but less critical tasks, allowing him to focus on strategic planning and making high-impact decisions, ultimately leading to the successful execution of the D-Day invasion.

Takeaway: Using the Eisenhower Matrix can help you differentiate between tasks that are genuinely important and those that only feel urgent. This distinction is crucial for busy entrepreneurs who often get caught up in putting out fires instead of working on what truly matters.

How to Use the Eisenhower Matrix:

1. **Create Your Matrix:**
   Draw a two-by-two grid with "Urgent" and "Not Urgent" on the top and "Important" and "Not Important" on the sides.

2. **Categorize Your Tasks:**
   Place your tasks into the appropriate quadrant.

3. **Act Accordingly:**
   Tackle urgent and important tasks first, schedule important but not urgent tasks, delegate urgent but not important tasks, and eliminate non-urgent, unimportant tasks.

THE IVY LEE METHOD: SIMPLIFYING YOUR DAY

In 1918, productivity consultant Ivy Lee was hired by Charles M. Schwab, CEO of Bethlehem Steel, to help his executives become more effective. By 1918, Charles M. Schwab was one of the richest men in the world. Schwab was the president of the Bethlehem Steel Corporation, the largest shipbuilder and the second-largest steel producer in America at the time. The famous inventor Thomas Edison once referred to Schwab as the "master hustler." He was constantly seeking an edge over the competition.

One day in 1918, in his quest to increase the efficiency of his team and discover better ways to get things done, Schwab arranged a meeting with a highly respected productivity consultant named Ivy Lee. Lee was a successful businessman in his own right and is widely remembered as a pioneer in the field of public relations. As the story goes, Schwab brought Lee into his office and said, "Show me a way to get more things done."

"Give me fifteen minutes with each of your executives," Lee replied.

"How much will it cost me?" Schwab asked.

"Nothing," Lee said. "Unless it works. After three months, you can send me a check for whatever you feel it's worth to you."

Lee's simple technique revolutionized their productivity:

1. At the end of each day, write down the six most important tasks you need to accomplish the next day.
2. Rank these tasks in order of importance.
3. The next day, start with the first task and work on it until it's completed before moving on to the next one.
4. Repeat this process every day.

The Ivy Lee Method forces you to prioritize your most important tasks and prevents you from spreading your attention across too many things at once.

WHY THIS METHOD WORKS FOR ADHD ENTREPRENEURS

For those with ADHD, having a structured plan with a limited number of tasks can reduce overwhelm and provide a clear direction for the day. It helps eliminate decision fatigue and keeps you focused on completing the most critical tasks first.

When Schwab implemented this method, Bethlehem Steel became the largest independent steel producer in the world. Schwab credited this simple prioritization technique as a key factor in the company's success.

USING TIME BLOCKING TO PRIORITIZE TASKS

Time blocking is a time management technique through which you schedule specific blocks of time for different tasks or activities throughout your day. This helps you dedicate focused time to high-priority tasks without interruptions. It helps people like me who are visually oriented, because I can see the whole block of time instead of just a line item written horizontally on a calendar.

For example, if I see "doctor appointment" written down at 2:00, I might not leave the house on time and also might schedule something else too soon after the appointment and end up rushed or late. Realistically, a doctor appointment block would be 1:15–3:30. That allows for enough time to drive, park, fill out paperwork, and sit longer than you expected in the waiting room or exam room.

How to Implement Time Blocking:

1. **Plan Your Day in Advance:**
   At the end of each day, review your to-do list and decide what tasks need time blocks for the next day.

2. **Assign Time Blocks:**
   Allocate specific time slots for each task, starting with your most important ones. For instance, you might block off 9:00–11:00 a.m. for deep work and 2:00–3:00 p.m. for meetings.

3. **Stick to the Schedule:**
   Treat your time blocks like appointments. Resist the urge to multitask or get sidetracked.

ELON MUSK: THE MASTER OF TIME BLOCKING

Elon Musk is a huge advocate of time blocking. Despite managing multiple companies like Tesla and SpaceX, he breaks his day into 5-minute time blocks, allowing him to focus intensely on specific tasks. This meticulous scheduling enables him to juggle massive responsibilities while maintaining high productivity.

Takeaway: Time blocking can help you set aside dedicated time for your most important tasks, reducing the chance of distractions and helping you stay on track.

ALIGNING YOUR PRIORITIES WITH YOUR LONG-TERM GOALS

It's easy to get caught up in daily tasks and lose sight of your bigger goals. One of the most effective ways to ensure your priorities are aligned is by using the **"Big Rocks" method**, a concept popularized by Stephen Covey.

1. **Identify Your Big Rocks:**
   These are the major goals or projects that are most important in your life and business.

2. **Schedule the Big Rocks First:**
   Put these priorities in your calendar before anything else. This ensures that you're making progress on your most important goals each week.

3. **Fill in with Smaller Tasks:**
   Once your big rocks are scheduled, you can fill in the remaining time with smaller, less critical tasks.

Example: The Big Rocks Jar Experiment

Covey often illustrated this concept with a jar, rocks, pebbles, and sand. The rocks represent your most important tasks, the pebbles are secondary tasks, and the sand is everything else. If you fill the jar with sand and pebbles first, the rocks won't fit. But if you start with the rocks, and then add pebbles and sand, everything fits perfectly. This demonstrates the importance of tackling your biggest priorities first.

Practical Exercise: Prioritization Planner

1. **Create a Master Task List:**
   Write down everything you need to accomplish for the week.

2. **Categorize Tasks:**
   Use the Eisenhower Matrix to categorize your tasks.

3. **Select Your Top Three Priorities for Each Day:**
   Focus on completing these tasks first before moving on to others.

4. **Reflect Weekly:**
   Review your progress at the end of each week. What worked well? What could be improved? Adjust your approach as needed.

ACTION STEPS TO MASTER PRIORITIZATION

1. **Apply the Pareto Principle:**
   Regularly review your tasks and identify the 20% that will yield 80% of the results.

2. **Use the Eisenhower Matrix:**
   Categorize your tasks using this tool to focus on what's important.

3. **Identify and Focus on HITs:**
   Choose 2–3 high-impact tasks each day and work on them first.

4. **Learn to Say No:**
   Protect your time and energy by declining tasks that don't align with your priorities.

By mastering the art of prioritization, you can ensure that your time and energy are spent on tasks that truly move your business forward. The goal is not just to be busy, but to be busy with the right things, ultimately transforming your focus into fortune.

PRIORITIZING PROFIT FIRST:
A STRATEGIC APPROACH TO BUSINESS GROWTH

"Profit is the result of focus, innovation, and perseverance."

— John Rampton

For many entrepreneurs, the most immediate and urgent tasks are often related to daily operations or client demands. However, focusing solely on these tasks can leave you scrambling for cash flow and struggling to grow your business sustainably. Prioritizing profit first means strategically placing profit-generating activities at the top of your to-do list to ensure your business remains healthy and continues to grow.

THE PROFIT FIRST MINDSET

The concept of "**Profit First**" was popularized by entrepreneur and author Mike Michalowicz in his book *Profit First*. He argues that rather than considering profit as what's left after expenses, businesses should treat profit as the primary goal. By prioritizing profit from the start, entrepreneurs can ensure their business remains financially healthy and sustainable.

Key Principle: *Revenue - Profit = Expenses*. Instead of the traditional accounting formula in which revenue minus expenses equals profit, this method forces you to focus on profitability first, allocating funds for profit before addressing expenses.

Steps to Prioritize Profit First:

1. **Identify Your Profit-Generating Activities:**
    Make a list of tasks that directly impact your revenue, such as sales calls, marketing campaigns, product launches, and client meetings. These are your high-priority tasks.

2. **Implement a Profit Allocation System:**
    Set aside a percentage of your revenue for profit as soon as it comes in. For example, allocate 10% of your income to a profit account before paying expenses. This forces you to make strategic decisions about spending and prioritize revenue-generating activities.

3. **Track and Analyze Profit Margins:**
    Regularly review your products or services to assess which ones offer the highest profit margins. Focus your efforts on promoting and improving these high-margin offerings to maximize profitability.

4. **Prioritize High-ROI Tasks Daily:**
    Make it a habit to tackle tasks that have a high return on investment (ROI) first. For example, instead of spending time on minor administrative tasks in

the morning, start your day with actions that directly lead to sales, such as following up with leads or launching a marketing campaign.

HOW SARA BLAKELY BUILT SPANX BY PRIORITIZING PROFIT

Sara Blakely, the founder of Spanx, was an early adopter of prioritizing profit in her business strategy. Before launching her product, she focused intensely on generating sales and maintaining a high profit margin by keeping her operations lean. She did not invest heavily in overhead or unnecessary expenses until she had proven that her product was profitable. By making profit a priority from the beginning, she was able to bootstrap her company and eventually turn it into a billion-dollar business without taking outside investment.

Takeaway: By prioritizing profit first, Sara Blakely avoided common pitfalls like overspending on non-essential expenses and ensured her business was financially healthy from the start.

Action Plan: Applying the Profit First Principle

Step 1: Create a Dedicated Profit Account
- Open a separate bank account specifically for profit. This simple step creates a visual reminder of your commitment to prioritizing profit.

Step 2: Allocate a Percentage of Revenue to Profit
- Decide on a fixed percentage of every payment you receive that will be transferred immediately to the profit account. Start small, if necessary, even 1–2%, and gradually increase it.

Step 3: Schedule Profit Review Sessions
- At the end of each month or quarter, review your profit account. Use these funds strategically for business investments, debt reduction, or reinvestment in growth activities.

Step 4: Prioritize Revenue-Generating Tasks

- As you plan your daily schedule, make sure that your highest priority is given to activities that have a direct impact on increasing sales and revenue. This could mean reaching out to potential clients, launching a marketing campaign, or refining a product that has high market demand.

INSPIRATION TO ACT NOW

"Success is not final; failure is not fatal:
it is the courage to continue that counts."

— Winston Churchill

The journey to mastering prioritization is ongoing. It requires consistent effort and the courage to make difficult choices about where to focus your time. Remember, prioritization is not about doing more things faster; it's about doing the right things with intention. By aligning your daily activities with your long-term goals, you set yourself on the path to sustainable growth and profitability.

CONCLUSION: TURNING PRIORITIZATION INTO A HABIT

"The secret of getting ahead is getting started. The secret of
getting started is breaking your complex, overwhelming tasks
into small manageable tasks, and then starting on the first one."

— Mark Twain

Mastering prioritization is about making deliberate choices that align with your goals. By implementing these strategies, you can create a clear path to success, focus on what matters most, and achieve greater productivity and profitability in your business.

Prioritizing profit first is not just an accounting strategy—it's a mindset shift. When you start prioritizing profit in your daily tasks and strategic decisions, you ensure that your business remains not only productive but also profitable. It's about making intentional choices that drive growth, allowing you to achieve financial stability and long-term success.

By incorporating a profit-first mentality into your prioritization process, you set a strong foundation for a thriving business. This approach helps you navigate your daily tasks with a clear focus on activities that will move your business forward and maximize your profitability. Focus on being productive instead of being busy.

CHAPTER 5

Protecting Your Time: Saying No Without Guilt and Setting Strong Boundaries

INTRODUCTION: THE POWER OF PROTECTING YOUR TIME

"You have to decide what your highest priorities are and have the courage—pleasantly, smilingly, unapologetically —to say no to other things. And the way you do that is by having a bigger yes burning inside."

— Stephen Covey

As an entrepreneur, your time is your most valuable asset. Yet, it's also the most vulnerable to external demands, distractions, and the expectations of others. The ability to say "no" without guilt and to set firm boundaries is not just about preserving your schedule—it's about prioritizing your well-being, maintaining your focus, and dedicating your energy to tasks that align with your goals.

In this chapter, we'll explore why saying no is a powerful productivity tool, how to set healthy boundaries, and strategies to protect your time effectively, even if you struggle with people-pleasing tendencies.

THE COST OF SAYING YES TO EVERYTHING

Many entrepreneurs and creative professionals find it hard to say no. The fear of missing out, the desire to please others, and the pressure to seize every opportunity can lead to overcommitment. But every time you say "yes" to something that doesn't align with your goals, you're effectively saying "no" to something more important.

Overcommitment is the commitment of your time and energy BEYOND what you have available and tricking yourself into thinking that somehow it will magically all work out, which often creates stress, exhaustion, and anxiety. Many people jam-pack their schedules because they keep adding things without letting go of anything. They fool themselves into thinking they will have plenty of time. Ultimately, this is the path to burnout.

Whether or not it appears evident at first, there is a high cost to having an overcommitted schedule. Some people find themselves robbing their personal lives to compensate for overcommitment at work. Being habitually late and rushed creates a high level of stress. There is often chronic fatigue because there is never enough time for sleep.

Some people can become addicted to stress and drama. They love the dopamine rush of being under the gun and have difficulty setting limits on the demands of others. Many have chronic anxiety because their life feels out of control, and they can't find balance in their lives.

An unbalanced life can feel draining. We all just have twenty-four hours in a day. When a professional runs out of time at work, they may steal that time from somewhere else to compensate. The extra time may be taken away from a marital relationship, exercise, friendships, family life, sleep, spiritual activities, or any of the other activities that make up a healthy, balanced life.

Ultimately, when you say "yes" to everyone, you are saying "no" to yourself. No matter what the choice is, you feel like you are letting someone down. And it is usually yourself, as you deprive yourself of sleep and relaxation and enjoyment, jumping through hoops, trying to please people, and juggling all of your competing demands. It is like the clown often seen with the plates spinning on sticks. Each time he goes to one side to steady one that is in danger of toppling, one starts to wobble on the other side. It is hard to keep them all spinning without one falling and cracking.

STEVE JOBS: THE ART OF FOCUSED SAYING NO

Steve Jobs was known for his relentless focus on saying no. When he returned to Apple in 1997, he cut down the product line from 350 items to just 10. He believed that focus was about saying no to hundreds of good ideas so that the company could fully commit to a few great ones. Jobs famously said, "I'm as proud of what we don't do as I am of what we do." His ability to say no was key to Apple's resurgence and success.

Takeaway: By learning to say no effectively, you create space for the projects and activities that truly matter, increasing your productivity and driving better results.

WHY WE STRUGGLE TO SAY NO

Understanding why saying no is so difficult can help you address this challenge head-on. Here are a few common reasons:

1. **Fear of Disappointment:**
    We worry that saying no will let others down or harm our relationships. We worry about what people will think of us.

2. **FOMO (Fear of Missing Out):**
    We fear missing out on potential opportunities, fun, networking, or experiences that could be beneficial.

3. **Desire to Please:**
    Many people, especially those with ADHD, may have a heightened desire to be helpful and accepted, leading them to say yes even when it's not in their best interest. All of us want to be liked by people, but many adults with ADHD have learned to jump through hoops to please people as a way to compensate for their ADHD struggles. People pleasers agree to do things for others when

they ask even at personal expense, such as being exhausted or already too busy. And what makes it worse is that the more they overcommit, the more forgetful and disorganized they become, and then they try to compensate through overcommitment. It's a vicious circle.

4. **Unclear Priorities:**
Without clear priorities, it's hard to evaluate whether an opportunity is worth your time, leading to overcommitment. I've heard it said that for adults with ADHD, it's as if life is a giant buffet and their eyes are always bigger than their stomachs.

5. **Impulsivity:**
This is a common trait of adults with ADHD, but many others struggle with it as well. And this impulsivity leads them to dive in headfirst without carefully considering other commitments they have already made. And for many entrepreneurs, they've done it this way for so long that it has become their M.O. They've crammed so many things into their lives so many times that it just feels normal to them.

LEARNING TO SAY NO: PROTECTING YOUR TIME

"When you say yes to everything, you are saying no to yourself."

— Cindy Baker

For many entrepreneurs, the hardest part of prioritization is learning to say no. We often feel obligated to say yes to every opportunity, meeting, or request for help, fearing that saying no will result in missed chances or lost relationships. However, the truth is that saying yes to everything dilutes your focus and reduces your effectiveness.

Why do we do this? Why do we so easily get overcommitted in our schedules? Many of us impulsively say "yes" as a knee-jerk reaction without stopping to consider the cost. And as pointed out earlier, there is a high cost to having an overcommitted schedule. Exhaustion, conflicts at home, and resentment toward others can occur. Some of us are people pleasers and say "yes" to gain approval. And some of us just have F.O.M.O. (fear of missing out). But the truth is, when you say yes to everyone, you are saying no to yourself. And you will always feel like you are letting someone down—and that someone is usually you.

THE STORY OF OPRAH WINFREY: THE POWER OF NO

Oprah Winfrey, one of the most influential women in media, has spoken openly about her struggle with saying no early in her career. She felt that saying no would disappoint people and harm her reputation. However, as her career progressed, she realized that constantly saying yes led to overwhelm and exhaustion.

Having a history of abuse meant she had trouble setting boundaries. Once your personal boundaries have been violated as a child, it's difficult to gather the courage to stop people from walking on you. She explained that you fear being rejected for who you really are. For years she ran herself ragged trying to fulfill other people's expectations of what she should do and who she should be. This proved to be an exhausting way to live.

Eventually, Oprah learned to value her time and started saying no to opportunities that didn't align with her goals. This change allowed her to focus on the projects she was truly passionate about, such as launching her own television network, writing books, and starting impactful philanthropic initiatives.

Takeaway: Protecting your time is crucial for maintaining productivity and avoiding burnout. Learning to say no, even to good opportunities, is essential for staying focused on your most important goals.

Tips for Saying No Gracefully:

1. **Be Clear on Your Priorities:**
    Knowing your goals makes it easier to recognize when to say no.

2. **Offer an Alternative:**
   If you feel uncomfortable saying no directly, suggest a different solution or recommend someone else who might help.

3. **Practice Polite Decline Phrases:**
   Use phrases like "I appreciate the offer, but I'm focusing on other projects right now" to decline politely.

THE ART OF SAYING NO WITHOUT GUILT

Learning to say no gracefully is a skill that can save you time, reduce stress, and help you stay focused on your most important tasks. Here are some strategies to make it easier:

1. **The Polite Decline**
   When faced with a request that doesn't align with your goals, use a polite but firm response:

   Example: "Thank you so much for thinking of me. I'm currently focusing on a few key projects, so I won't be able to take this on right now."

   This approach acknowledges the request while clearly stating your boundaries.

2. **Offer an Alternative**
   If you want to decline without shutting the door completely, suggest an alternative that requires less of your time:

   Example: "I can't join the committee, but I'd be happy to review the proposal and give feedback when I have some time next week."

   This shows your willingness to help while setting a limit on your involvement.

3. **Blame Your Schedule, Not Yourself**
   Deflect the blame onto your schedule to avoid feeling guilty:

Example: "I'd love to help, but my schedule is fully booked this week. Let's touch base again in a few weeks."

This makes it clear that your time is already committed, reducing the pressure to say yes.

4. **Use a "Soft No" with a "Hard Follow-Up"**
   Start with a soft no, leaving room for the requester to reconsider:

   Example: "I'm not sure I can commit to this right now. Let me think about it and get back to you."

   When you follow up, give a firm no if the request still doesn't align with your priorities.

QUALIFYING YOUR YES:

You do not have to always say "no." But you may need to start qualifying your "yes."

"Yes, if I can get someone else to take over my current project I'm working on…"

"Yes, I'd love to help but will have to wait until my calendar clears."

"Yes, I am very interested, and when my schedule clears a little, I'll let you know."

Don't just knee-jerk blurt out "yes" before you've had a chance to think through all the implications. Always pause and say, "I'm interested, but I need some time to think about it."

Don't let your enthusiasm get the better of you! Always take time to carefully consider everything first.

SETTING STRONG BOUNDARIES

Setting boundaries is essential for maintaining focus and protecting your time. Boundaries are like invisible walls that help you control how you spend your time and energy.

1. **Establish Work Hours and Stick to Them**
    Set specific hours when you are available for meetings, calls, or other work-related activities. Communicate these boundaries clearly to clients, colleagues, and even friends and family.

    Example: "I typically take calls between 1 p.m. and 4 p.m. Can we schedule our discussion during that window?"

    By setting expectations upfront, you can protect your focus during peak productivity hours.

2. **Create Physical and Digital Boundaries**

    Physical Boundaries:
    Designate a workspace that is free from distractions. If you work from home, let your household members know when you're not to be disturbed.

    Digital Boundaries:
    Limit access to your time through digital tools. Set "Do Not Disturb" modes on your devices, use email autoresponders, and disable notifications during deep work sessions.

3. **Practice Saying No to Yourself**
    Internal boundaries are just as important as external ones. Learn to say no to distractions like social media, unplanned tasks, and impulse decisions that can derail your productivity.

Tip: Use the **Pomodoro Technique** to set a timer for 25 minutes of focused work, followed by a 5-minute break. This can help you resist the urge to switch tasks and maintain focus.

4. **Use "Boundaries Scripts"**

Having a go-to script can make it easier to say no in the moment without feeling caught off guard. Here are some examples:

- **For Interruptions:**
  "I'm in the middle of something important right now. Can we catch up later?"

- **For Unsolicited Requests:**
  "That sounds like a great opportunity, but I have to pass right now to focus on my current commitments."

- **For Persistent Requests:**
  "I've given this some thought, and I need to prioritize other projects at this time. I appreciate your understanding."

ACTION PLAN: START PRACTICING THE POWER OF NO

1. **Identify Your Top Priorities:**
   Write down your top three goals for the next quarter. Use these as your guiding principles when deciding whether to accept or decline requests.

2. **Create Your Personal "No Script":**
   Draft a few polite ways to say no. Practice these scripts so you feel comfortable using them when needed.

3. **Schedule "No" Reviews:**
   At the end of each week, review your calendar and tasks. Did you overcommit? Use this reflection to improve your ability to say no in the future.

CONCLUSION: EMBRACE THE FREEDOM OF SAYING NO

"Half of the troubles of this life can be traced to saying yes too quickly and not saying no soon enough."

— Josh Billings

Saying no is a powerful act of self-respect. It allows you to set boundaries, protect your time, and focus on what truly matters. By mastering this skill, you can take control of your schedule, reduce stress, and create space for the work that brings you closer to your goals. Remember, every time you say no to a lesser priority, you are saying yes to what truly counts.

CHAPTER 6

Building Productive
Routines and Habits for Lasting Success

INTRODUCTION: THE POWER OF CONSISTENCY

*"Success is the sum of small efforts, repeated
day in and day out."*

— Robert Collier

As an entrepreneur, it's easy to feel overwhelmed by the sheer number of tasks you need to juggle. However, consistent habits and routines are the backbone of productivity. Successful entrepreneurs don't rely on motivation alone; they build systems and habits that allow them to stay on track, no matter how they feel on any given day.

This chapter will explore how establishing effective routines and habits can streamline your day, reduce decision fatigue, and ultimately help you achieve your goals with less effort. We'll dive into the science of habit formation and show you how to leverage **habit stacking** to create a foundation for sustainable productivity and success.

THE SCIENCE OF HABIT FORMATION

Habits are powerful because they automate behavior. Once a habit is established, it requires less cognitive energy to execute, freeing up your brain to focus on more complex tasks. According to research, it takes around sixty-six days for a new behavior to become automatic, but this can vary depending on the individual and the complexity of the habit.

WHY ROUTINES AND HABITS MATTER FOR ENTREPRENEURS

Routines and habits are crucial for several reasons:

1. **Reduce Mental Energy:**
    Each decision you make, from what to eat to what task to prioritize, drains your mental energy. Establishing routines reduces this mental load, allowing you to conserve your willpower for important decisions.

2. **Increase Consistency:**
    Consistency breeds results. By following a routine, you're setting yourself up for steady progress, even on days when motivation is low.

3. **Boost Efficiency:**
    With the right habits in place, you can complete tasks more quickly and with less effort, freeing up time for other important activities.

4. **Create Structure:**
    Routines provide structure in your day, which is especially valuable for individuals with ADHD, who may struggle with time management and staying organized.

BUILDING YOUR ROUTINE: KEY ELEMENTS FOR ENTREPRENEURIAL SUCCESS

To build a productive routine, it's essential to start with a solid framework that aligns with your goals and priorities. Here are some key elements to incorporate into your daily routine:

1. **Start Your Day with Intention**

   How you start your day sets the tone for the rest of it. Instead of jumping straight into emails or social media, create a morning routine that prioritizes focus and clarity.

Example Morning Routine:

- Wake up at the same time each day.
- Practice 5–10 minutes of prayer, mindfulness, or meditation.
- Set your intention for the day (write down your top three goals).
- Get moving with light exercise or stretching.
- Eat a healthy, energizing breakfast.
- Review your schedule and prioritize your tasks.

By creating a morning routine, you create a predictable start to your day, which reduces stress and allows you to dive into work with focus.

2. **Block Time for Deep Work**

   Deep work refers to the state of focused, undistracted work that allows you to accomplish high-impact tasks. Schedule dedicated blocks of time for deep work, ideally during your peak energy hours.

   Tip: Use the **Pomodoro Technique**—work for 25 minutes, followed by a 5-minute break. This method helps maintain focus while preventing burnout.

3. **Regular Breaks and Self-Care**

   Building regular breaks into your routine is critical for maintaining long-term productivity. Without breaks, you risk burnout and diminishing returns.

Example Break Routine:

- 5-minute breaks after every 25 minutes of work (Pomodoro method)
- 30-minute lunch break away from your workspace
- At least one hour of physical activity or relaxation each day

4. **Evening Reflection and Wind-Down Routine**
   End your day by reflecting on your achievements and preparing for the next day. This not only helps you feel accomplished but also ensures you're ready to hit the ground running tomorrow.

Evening Routine:

- Review what you accomplished during the day.
- Set your top priorities for tomorrow.
- Unplug from digital devices an hour before bed.
- Practice relaxation techniques to wind down (e.g., reading, light stretching, journaling).

This wind-down routine signals to your body that it's time to rest, which can improve your sleep quality and help you start the next day refreshed.

HABITS: THE SMALL ACTIONS THAT LEAD TO BIG RESULTS

"Successful people are simply those with successful habits."

— Brian Tracy

While routines provide structure, **habits** are the building blocks that support your overall productivity and well-being. Here's how to start building habits that stick:

1. **Focus on One Habit at a Time**
   Trying to overhaul your entire routine at once can be overwhelming. Start small, focusing on one habit at a time. Once that habit is ingrained, you can move on to the next one.

   Example: If you want to build a habit of exercise, start by committing to just ten minutes of physical activity per day. Gradually increase the duration as the habit becomes more automatic.

2. **Use the 2-Minute Rule**

   If a task feels overwhelming, use the 2-Minute Rule: If a habit or task can be done in two minutes or less, do it immediately. This simple rule prevents procrastination and helps you tackle small tasks that would otherwise pile up.

   Example: Instead of leaving emails unread in your inbox, read and respond to short ones right away.

3. **Track Your Progress**

   Tracking your progress is a powerful motivator. Use a habit-tracking app or a simple calendar to mark off each day you successfully complete a habit. This creates a visual reminder of your success, which reinforces the habit.

   Tip: Celebrate your small wins! Positive reinforcement can make the habit stick even faster.

HABIT STACKING: MAKING NEW HABITS STICK

Habit stacking is a technique developed by BJ Fogg in his book *Tiny Habits*. It involves taking a habit you already do and stacking a new habit on top of it. This makes the new habit easier to remember and implement because it's tied to an existing routine.

How Habit Stacking Works
To stack a habit, follow this simple formula:

"After [current habit], I will [new habit]."

For example:

- **Current habit:**
  After I brush my teeth, I will write down my top three tasks for the day.

- **Current habit:**
  After I finish my morning coffee, I will spend 20 minutes on deep work.

By linking a new habit to an existing one, you're using the power of association to reinforce the new behavior, making it easier to integrate into your life.

Examples of Habit Stacking:
- **Morning routine stack:**
  After I wake up, I will drink a glass of water. After drinking water, I will journal for 5 minutes.

- **Productivity stack:**
  After I check my email in the morning, I will immediately start on the top task of my to-do list for 30 minutes.

Habit stacking works because it leverages your existing habits, reducing the mental effort needed to create new routines. The key is consistency—stick to your stacked habits until they become automatic.

HOW BENJAMIN FRANKLIN USED HABITS FOR SUCCESS

Benjamin Franklin, one of America's Founding Fathers, was famous for his use of routines and habits to achieve great success. He created a daily schedule that balanced his work, self-improvement, and rest. One of his most notable habits was his focus on **virtue**, which he categorized into thirteen different areas of life, such as order, silence, and industry. Each day, Franklin would assess his behavior and track his progress in these areas.

Takeaway: Franklin's use of habits wasn't about perfection—it was about continuous improvement. His commitment to his daily routines and habits led him to become one of the most productive and influential individuals in history.

Action Plan: Building and Stacking Your Own Habits

1. **Identify Your Core Routine:**
   Write down your current routine. Where can you add new, productive habits that will support your goals?

2. **Choose One Habit to Stack:**
   Pick one habit you want to build and stack it onto an existing habit.

3. **Track Your Progress:**
   Use a habit tracker or journal to mark your progress each day. Celebrate small wins to stay motivated.

4. **Reassess Monthly:**
   At the end of each month, reflect on your habits. Which ones are helping you progress toward your goals? Which ones need tweaking?

CONCLUSION: SMALL HABITS, BIG RESULTS

"Your habits will determine your future."

— Jack Canfield

Building productive routines and habits doesn't happen overnight. It requires patience, consistency, and self-compassion. But with small, daily actions, you'll create a foundation for success that will serve you for years to come. By habit stacking, tracking progress, and staying focused on your priorities, you can transform your day, your business, and your life.

Let these habits and routines be the structure that supports your entrepreneurial journey—helping you stay productive, focused, and ultimately more successful.

CHAPTER 7

Achieving Life Balance by Aligning Your Time with What Truly Matters

INTRODUCTION: THE POWER OF LIFE BALANCE

"Never get so busy making a living that you forget to make a life."

— Dolly Parton

As an entrepreneur, you're often pulled in a million directions—balancing your business, your personal life, your health, and your relationships. The demands can feel relentless, leaving little time for rest, reflection, or the things that bring you joy. But without balance, even the most successful business can start to feel hollow.

In this chapter, we'll explore the concept of life balance, not as a perfect equilibrium between work and personal life, but as a dynamic state where your time reflects your values and your vision for your life. When you stop doing the things that don't truly matter and start prioritizing what's most important to you, you create a life that is both meaningful and productive.

THE MYTH OF PERFECT BALANCE

Many entrepreneurs struggle with the idea of achieving perfect balance, often imagining that life should consist of an equal distribution of time between work, personal life, and relaxation. However, this is a myth. True life balance isn't about equal allocation—it's about alignment. It's about recognizing where your time is going and deciding whether it aligns with your values and what matters most to you.

Balance isn't static. Some seasons of life will demand more focus on work, while other times will require you to prioritize family, health, or rest. The key is understanding where you are in each season and making intentional choices about how you spend your time.

Step 1: Defining What Matters Most to You

To achieve life balance, you must first identify what truly matters to you. What are your core values? What do you want your life to stand for?

Exercise: Clarify Your Values

Take some time to reflect on these questions:

- What values do I hold most dear (e.g., family, health, creativity, contribution, independence)?

- When I look back on my life, what do I want to have accomplished (e.g., building a successful business, raising children, traveling the world, impacting others)?

- What brings me joy and fulfillment outside of work (e.g., spending time with loved ones, hobbies, spiritual practices, outdoor activities)?

Write down your answers. Your values might include things like:

- **Family:** Spending quality time with loved ones
- **Health:** Prioritizing physical and mental well-being
- **Creativity:** Pursuing artistic or innovative endeavors
- **Growth:** Investing in personal and professional development
- **Contribution:** Giving back to your community or making a difference in the world

Once you identify your values, you'll have a clearer understanding of how to prioritize your time. These values will act as your compass, helping you make decisions about where to invest your energy.

Step 2: Letting Go of What Doesn't Matter

Once you've identified your core values, it's time to let go of the things that no longer serve your priorities. It's easy to become distracted by obligations, commitments, and "shoulds" "that pull you away from what matters most.

The Power of Saying No

As mentioned before, one of the most powerful skills you can develop is the ability to say "no" without guilt. When you say yes to something that doesn't align with your values, you are saying no to something that does.

Example: You might feel obligated to attend social events or take on additional projects, but if those commitments take time away from your family or personal well-being, they may not be worth your energy. Learning to say no allows you to reserve your time for what truly aligns with your vision for your life.

"You have to say no to the good so you can say yes to the best."

— John C. Maxwell

Exercise: Evaluate Your Commitments

Review your calendar for the past month. Identify areas where you spent time on things that didn't serve your core values. Ask yourself:

- Was this activity or commitment aligned with my values?
- Did I feel drained or energized by this activity?
- Was it truly necessary, or was it something I felt obligated to do?

Use these questions to evaluate your current commitments. If something doesn't align with your core values, consider letting it go.

Step 3: Designing Your Ideal Schedule

Now that you've identified your values and removed the distractions, it's time to design a schedule that reflects what truly matters.

The Importance of Prioritization

Your schedule should be a reflection of your priorities. Here's how you can align your time with your values:

1. **Time Block for What Matters:**
   - If health is a priority, block out time for exercise or relaxation.
   - If family is a priority, set aside dedicated time for them—whether it's family dinners or weekend outings.
   - If creativity is a priority, schedule time each day to engage in creative work.

2. **Use the Eisenhower Matrix for Prioritization:**
   The Eisenhower Matrix helps you prioritize tasks based on urgency and importance:

   - **Urgent and Important:**
     These tasks need to be done immediately. Examples: client deadlines, urgent family matters.

   - **Not Urgent but Important:**
     These tasks are important for long-term success but aren't urgent. Examples: personal development, strategic planning, family time.

   - **Urgent but Not Important:**
     These tasks might seem urgent, but they don't significantly impact your long-term goals. Example: emails, low-priority meetings.

- **Not Urgent and Not Important:**
  These tasks should be minimized or eliminated. Example: time spent on distractions, unnecessary tasks.

3. **Incorporate Flexibility:**
   Life is unpredictable, and true balance includes flexibility. Set aside buffer time in your schedule for unexpected events or relaxation.

Exercise: Design Your Weekly Schedule
- Look at the hours in your week and block out time for the things that matter most: health, family, creativity, business, and relaxation.
- Make sure that your schedule reflects your core values, not just your to-do list.
- Don't forget to schedule downtime. Your body and mind need time to recharge.

Step 4: Creating Boundaries and Protecting Your Time

Once you've aligned your schedule with your values, it's crucial to protect your time. This means setting boundaries with others and yourself.

Setting Boundaries with Clients and Colleagues

As an entrepreneur, you may feel pressure to always be available. But to maintain life balance, you need to set clear boundaries around your working hours.

- **Tip:** Let your clients know when you're available and when you're not. Set expectations for response times and honor your own time outside of work.
- **Tip:** Create an "off-the-clock" routine where you step away from work entirely—no checking emails or taking calls outside of designated work hours.

Setting Boundaries with Yourself

Just as you set boundaries with others, you also need to set boundaries with yourself. It's easy to fall into the trap of overworking, especially when you're passionate about your business.

Tip: Use productivity techniques like time blocking or the Pomodoro Technique to prevent overworking. Set clear limits for work tasks and stick to them.

Step 5: Regularly Reflect and Adjust

Life balance is a dynamic process, not a one-time achievement. Over time, your priorities may shift, and so should your schedule. Make it a habit to regularly reflect on your life balance:

- **Monthly Reflection:**
  At the end of each month, review your schedule. Are you spending enough time on the things that matter most? Is anything creeping in that shouldn't be there? Adjust accordingly.

- **Quarterly Check-In:**
  Every few months, reassess your values and your life goals. Are you on track? Are there new priorities you want to focus on?

CONCLUSION: LIVING A LIFE OF INTENTIONAL BALANCE

"The key is not to prioritize what's on your schedule, but to schedule your priorities."

— Stephen Covey

Achieving life balance is about aligning your time with what truly matters to you. It's about designing a life that supports your values, gives you the freedom to focus on what's important, and creates space for rest, rejuvenation, and joy. By regularly evaluating your commitments, saying no to distractions, and creating a schedule that reflects your deepest priorities, you'll unlock the ability to live a fulfilling life both personally and professionally.

The journey toward life balance isn't linear, but with intention, clarity, and the courage to protect your time, you can create a life that not only reflects your values but also supports your entrepreneurial success.

CHAPTER 8

How Entrepreneurs with ADHD Experience Time Differently and How to Leverage Your Strengths

INTRODUCTION: THE ADHD TIME PARADOX

"Time flies over us but leaves its shadow behind."

— Nathaniel Hawthorne

Since I have ADHD, I wanted to add in this bonus chapter for all who share my experience. I read somewhere that over 60% of entrepreneurs have ADHD. I do not know if that statistic is correct or not, but I do know that even if you do not have ADHD, chances are you may work with someone who does. Either way, it is helpful to understand the connection between ADHD and time management.

Entrepreneurs with ADHD often experience time in a unique way. For many, time doesn't feel like a steady stream but more like a fluctuating force that moves quickly in some moments and drags on in others. This can be both a challenge and a strength—depending on how it is managed.

In this chapter, we'll explore how ADHD entrepreneurs experience time differently from others, how the "now or not now" mentality can impact productivity, and how to leverage ADHD strengths, such as hyperfocus, to achieve extraordinary results in your business.

UNDERSTANDING THE ADHD EXPERIENCE OF TIME

People with ADHD often feel like they live in two states of time: *now* and *not now*. When a task is urgent or captivating, time feels like it's moving at lightning speed— this is often referred to as hyperfocus. But when something feels uninteresting or overwhelming, time seems to slow down, making it hard to get started or stay on task. It is hard to focus on long-term priorities when you are continuously caught up in the stimulus of your immediate experience in the *now*.

Only the things in an ADHD person's immediate experience get attention, whether they are a priority or not. Even if something has been planned ahead of time and written on a planner, it gets little or no attention in comparison to the "now" of a phone notification or something you see out the window or hear in the other room. If I have a project due in three months, my brain automatically says, "Oh, that's not now. I don't have to think about it." But then when the deadline approaches, I may panic because I did not break the large task up into manageable mini-tasks and work on it a little along the way leading up to the deadline. Living this way continuously can result in depression, toxic worry, and anxiety.

"In ADD, time collapses, making life feel as if everything is happening at once. This creates panic. We lose perspective and the ability to select what needs to be done first, second, another day, etc. Instead, you are always on the go, leaping before you look, always trying to keep the world from caving in on top of you. You live in overwhelm."

— From *Driven to Distraction* by Drs. Hallowell & Ratey

This experience can sometimes feel like a roller coaster of productivity. On the one hand, you can achieve remarkable focus and get things done in bursts of energy. On the other hand, there can be moments of procrastination, distraction, and difficulty in starting or completing tasks. But understanding this time dynamic can be the key to unlocking your productivity.

THE "NOW OR NOT NOW" MENTALITY

Let's explore this phenomenon a little closer. Entrepreneurs with ADHD often feel like they can only operate at full capacity in one of two modes: **Now** or **Not Now**. This often leads to periods of intense productivity (the "Now" phase) followed by periods of inaction or distraction (the "Not Now" phase). Understanding these patterns is key to managing time effectively.

- **The "Now" Mode:**
  When you're fully engaged and hyper-focused on a task, you may feel like time doesn't exist. You can work for hours without feeling the weight of deadlines or the passing of time. This is often referred to as "hyperfocus" and can be an incredibly powerful tool for productivity, especially when you can channel it toward tasks that truly matter.

- **The "Not Now" Mode:**
  On the flip side, there are times when getting started on a task feels impossible. The mind wanders, distractions pile up, and procrastination sets in. During these moments, it can feel like time is dragging, and you may struggle to get any meaningful work done.

But understanding that you experience time this way can actually be a huge advantage. Once you accept the "now or not now" dynamic, you can work with it instead of against it.

HYPERFOCUS: THE ADHD SUPERPOWER

One of the most significant advantages of ADHD is the ability to experience hyperfocus. Hyperfocus is a state in which an individual becomes intensely absorbed in an activity, often to the exclusion of everything else. When you're in this state, time seems to fly, and productivity soars.

Hyperfocus can be a powerful tool for entrepreneurs when harnessed correctly. Here's how you can leverage this strength to your advantage:

HOW TO LEVERAGE HYPERFOCUS FOR YOUR BUSINESS

1. **Identify Tasks That Trigger Hyperfocus:**
    Certain tasks or projects may naturally trigger your hyperfocus. For example, you might experience it when you're working on creative brainstorming, solving complex problems, or strategizing. Recognizing these triggers can help you plan your most demanding tasks during times when you're most likely to experience hyperfocus.

2. **Work in Short, Intense Bursts:**
    Rather than trying to pace yourself throughout the day, consider structuring your work in intense, time-limited bursts. Use techniques like the Pomodoro method (working for 25 minutes, then taking a 5-minute break) to create focused periods in which you can dive deeply into work. When you feel the urge to focus, seize the moment.

3. **Minimize Distractions:**
    Hyperfocus can be disrupted by external distractions, so create a distraction-free environment when you sense that focus is kicking in. Turn off notifications, close unnecessary tabs, and set up a space where you can concentrate fully.

4. **Use Hyperfocus to Solve Big Problems:**
    When you're in hyperfocus mode, your problem-solving abilities are amplified. This is the time to tackle complex tasks or projects that require deep thinking and attention to detail. Don't waste these moments on mundane tasks—save them for the most important and challenging work.

ALBERT EINSTEIN'S HYPERFOCUS

Albert Einstein is a prime example of someone who used his hyperfocus to change the world. It's said that Einstein could work for hours without being aware of time, losing himself in complex equations and theoretical physics. He was so absorbed in his work that he often forgot basic needs like eating or sleeping. This ability to hyperfocus allowed him to make groundbreaking discoveries, including his theory of relativity, which forever changed the course of science.

Like Einstein, you can harness the power of hyperfocus to achieve exceptional results, whether you're developing a new product, creating a marketing strategy, or working through a problem in your business.

MANAGING THE "NOT NOW" MODE: HOW TO GET UNSTUCK

While hyperfocus is a strength, the "Not Now" phase can be a challenge. When you're feeling stuck, time can seem to stand still, making it hard to get anything done. But by understanding how ADHD impacts your time perception, you can create strategies to combat procrastination and regain focus.

STRATEGIES TO BREAK FREE FROM "NOT NOW"

1. **Use Time Limits:**
   Instead of focusing on completing a task, give yourself a time limit. For example, tell yourself, "I'm going to work on this for 15 minutes," and set a timer. The pressure of a short, manageable time frame can help you break through inertia and get started.

2. **Start with the Easiest Task:**
   When everything feels overwhelming, start with the simplest task on your to-do list. This will give you a quick win and build momentum to tackle larger tasks.

3. **Use the 2-Minute Rule:**
   The 2-Minute Rule states that if something takes less than two minutes to complete, do it immediately. This rule helps you clear out small tasks quickly, so they don't pile up and create unnecessary mental clutter.

4. **Engage in Mindfulness:**
   Sometimes, the "Not Now" feeling is linked to anxiety or overwhelm. Mindfulness techniques can help you ground yourself and refocus. Take a few minutes to breathe deeply, meditate, or engage in some light stretching to center your mind before jumping back into work. Jot down any worries that pop into your head and put them in a "parking lot" such as a file or bulletin board to be dealt with later.

5. **Set Clear and Small Goals:**
   Break down tasks into smaller, manageable pieces. Instead of focusing on the entire project, focus on one small aspect you can achieve in the moment.

THE ADHD ADVANTAGE: TIME PERCEPTION AS A STRENGTH

While the "now or not now" mentality can create moments of chaos, it also provides a unique advantage for entrepreneurs with ADHD. When you understand how your brain experiences time, you can create systems that leverage these natural tendencies for maximum productivity.

Here's how you can turn your ADHD time experience into a business advantage:

1. **Create Time Blocks for Deep Work:**
   Use your hyperfocus to carve out blocks of uninterrupted time for important tasks. These periods of intense focus can lead to faster decision-making, more innovation, and greater productivity.

2. **Embrace Flexibility:**
   Because time feels fluid for those with ADHD, you might find it hard to stick to rigid schedules. Embrace flexible work hours and fluid planning. As long as you're meeting your key business objectives, it doesn't matter exactly *when* you achieve them.

3. **Embrace Creative Problem-Solving:**
Entrepreneurs with ADHD often have unique perspectives that allow them to see creative solutions to problems. Leverage your quick thinking and ability to see connections others might miss.

4. **Shift Your Mindset from Time Struggles to Time Mastery:**
Once you understand how time works for you, shift from a mindset of struggle to one of mastery. Focus on how you can use your strengths to achieve your goals, rather than trying to force yourself into a one-size-fits-all approach to time management.

RICHARD BRANSON AND TIME MASTERY

Richard Branson, the founder of the Virgin Group, is a well-known example of an ADHD entrepreneur who has mastered the art of managing time. Branson's business ventures are diverse, yet he's known for his ability to focus intensely on projects that excite him, all while maintaining a healthy work-life balance.

Branson has said, "I don't believe in limiting myself to one or two businesses. I've always said if you're good at something, it's easy to learn how to do the next thing. But you have to have the discipline to get started."

Branson uses his ADHD traits—creativity, energy, and the ability to hyperfocus—along with a flexible approach to time management to grow his empire while ensuring that he's always working on what excites him.

CONCLUSION: EMBRACE YOUR ADHD STRENGTHS TO MASTER TIME

"Time is what we want most but what we use worst."

— William Penn

As an ADHD entrepreneur, your relationship with time is unique. Understanding how you experience time—through hyperfocus and the "now or not now" mentality—can help you leverage your strengths to your advantage.

CONCLUSION: MASTERING TIME TO BUILD A PROFITABLE, PURPOSEFUL BUSINESS

"The time is always right to do what is right."

— Martin Luther King Jr.

Throughout this book, we've delved into the essential relationship between time management and business success. Whether you have ADHD or simply struggle with distractions, the principles we've covered are designed to help you regain control of your time, maximize your productivity, and grow your business. The strategies shared throughout this book aren't one-size-fits-all, but rather adaptable tools that cater to the unique needs of entrepreneurs who want to take charge of their time, their tasks, and ultimately, their lives.

Time can often feel like an elusive force—sometimes slipping through our fingers, other times feeling like it's dragging. Whether you are overwhelmed by a long to-do list or constantly battling interruptions, the power lies in how you manage and structure your time. The good news is, with the right approach, **time can become your most valuable asset in business and in life**.

EMBRACE YOUR STRENGTHS AND WORK WITH YOUR NATURAL RHYTHMS

No matter your struggles with distraction, the truth remains: **You have strengths.** The ability to hyperfocus, think outside the box, and tackle challenges head-on are all traits that can work in your favor—especially when you understand how to harness them. The key is to stop fighting against the distractions that come naturally and instead turn them into assets.

By leaning into what makes you unique—whether that's a creativity-driven focus or an adaptive ability to shift gears quickly—you can begin to work smarter, not harder. Successful entrepreneurs are not necessarily those who follow rigid time management techniques, but those who understand how to work with their own rhythms and create systems that align with their unique mindset.

TIME MANAGEMENT IS ABOUT MORE THAN JUST BUSINESS—IT'S ABOUT LIFE

The key takeaway from this book is simple: **Time is not just for business**. It's about aligning your time with what matters most to you in life. Profits are important, but they're not the only measure of success. Balancing your work with your personal life, relationships, and well-being is equally critical to living a fulfilling life.

By applying the techniques in this book, you've learned how to:

1. **Eliminate distractions** and design your environment to help you focus on what truly matters.
2. **Prioritize the tasks** that will have the most impact on your business and life.
3. **Set boundaries** and stop saying "yes" to everything that doesn't align with your core values.
4. **Create routines** and habits that set you up for success each day.
5. **Embrace balance** and design a schedule that reflects what is most important to you, both in your business and personal life.

START WHERE YOU ARE—AND BUILD MOMENTUM

As you finish this book, remember that the journey to mastering your time doesn't require perfection. Start by choosing one of the strategies that resonated with you—whether it's setting boundaries, implementing a morning routine, or using a productivity tool—and try it today. You don't need to overhaul everything at once; simply take small steps that align with your priorities, and you'll start seeing the difference.

Here's how you can begin:

1. **Pick one strategy to implement today:**
    Start small—whether it's creating a distraction-free workspace, scheduling "focus sprints," or saying no to a non-essential task. Action, no matter how small, leads to progress.

2. **Be consistent:**
    Over time, small shifts will compound into meaningful change. Keep applying these strategies, tweaking them as needed, and give yourself grace as you navigate your entrepreneurial journey.

3. **Celebrate your wins:**
    Whether it's completing a project on time, getting through a tough week without burnout, or simply recognizing that you're focusing on what matters most, every step forward counts.

YOUR TIME, YOUR BUSINESS, YOUR LIFE

At the end of the day, managing your time is about creating the life and business you've always wanted. By taking control of your time, prioritizing what truly matters, and setting boundaries around your work, you'll find that you have more space—space for creativity, space for personal time, and space to grow your business without sacrificing your health or relationships.

Remember, success is not only about what you achieve but how you achieve it. And that comes down to **how you choose to spend your time**. Whether it's focusing on high-impact tasks, saying no to distractions, or carving out time for self-care, each choice you make contributes to the overall success and well-being of your life and business.

FINAL THOUGHT: YOU HAVE THE POWER TO MAKE TIME WORK FOR YOU

"The good of being delivered from hurry is not simply pleasure but the ability to do calmly and effectively – with strength and joy – that which really matters."

— John Mark Comer

Time waits for no one, but you have the power to shape how you use it. By applying the strategies in this book, you can take back control of your time, work smarter, and achieve your entrepreneurial goals with less stress and more fulfillment. The journey doesn't end here—it's only just begun.

Now, go out and take the reins of your time. Your business, your life, and your future are waiting for you to make the most of them. You've got this!

Thank you for allowing me to guide you on this journey. I can't wait to see all that you accomplish with your newfound approach to time management.

References

Arthur Lawrence. "Steve Jobs' Top 10 Secret Tips for Insane Productivity."
Accessed February 24, 2025. https://www.arthurlawrence.net/blog/steve-jobs-insane-productivity-tips/?

Bareš, Jakub. "What Einstein Knew About ADHD." Metamatics, October 29,
2024. https://essays.metamatics.org/p/what-einstein-knew-about-adhd?utm_campaign=post&utm_medium=web

Chai, Wesley. "Eisenhower Matrix." TechTarget. Accessed February 24, 2025.
https://www.techtarget.com/whatis/definition/Eisenhower-Matrix?

Clear, James. "Atomic Habits." Accessed February 24, 2025.
https://jamesclear.com/atomic-habits.

Clear, James. "The Ivy Lee Method: The Daily Routine Experts Recommend for
Peak Productivity." Accessed February 24, 2025. https://jamesclear.com/ivy-lee?

Clear, James. "Warren Buffett's "2 List" Strategy: How to Maximize Your Focus
and Master Your Priorities." Accessed February 24, 2015.
https://jamesclear.com/buffett-focus.

Davies, Caroline. "From Aristotle to Einstein: A brief history of power nappers."
The Guardian, August 27, 2021.
https://www.theguardian.com/lifeandstyle/2021/aug/27/from-aristotle-to-einstein-a-brief-history-of-power-nappers.

Farnan Street. "The Focus to Say No." Blog. Accessed February 25, 2025.
https://fs.blog/steve-jobs-saying-no/.

Farnan Street. "Ben Franklin: The Thirteen Necessary Virtues." Blog. Accessed February 25, 2025. https://fs.blog/the-thirteen-virtues/.

Haden, Jeff. "Richard Branson on How to Pursue Your Dreams and Achieve More Without Time Management Tools." Inc., August 5, 2022. https://www.inc.com/jeff-haden/richard-branson-on-how-to-pursue-your-dreams-achieve-more-without-time-management-tools.html.

Hallowell, Edward M., and John J. Ratey. *Driven to Distraction: Recognizing and Coping with Attention Deficit Disorder from Childhood through Adulthood.* Touchstone, 1994.

History. "Benjamin Franklin." Last updated June 25, 2024. https://www.history.com/topics/american-revolution/benjamin-franklin.

Inc. "Steve Jobs Used the 30 Percent Rule to Bring Apple Back From the Dead (It'll Work for You, Too)." Accessed February 24, 2025. https://www.inc.com/justin-bariso/steve-jobs-used-30-percent-rule-to-bring-apple-back-from-dead-itll-work-for-you-too.html?

Jackson, Sarah. "Tim Cook's Daily Routine: The Schedule of the Apple CEO Who Wakes Up at 3:45 a.m. and Reads Hundreds of Customer Emails a Day." *Entrepreneur*, October 11, 2023. https://www.entrepreneur.com/business-news/apple-ceo-tim-cooks-routine-emails-meetings-energy-bars/463506.

Mental Garden. "Ivy Lee Method: The most effective minimalist productivity method." Blog. Medium, September 11, 2024. https://medium.com/%40mentalgarden/ivy-lee-method-the-most-effective-minimalist-productivity-method-94d87fbc8389.

Merle, Andrew. "The Importance of Blank Space on Your Calendar." Medium, November 27, 2018. https://andrewmerle.medium.com/the-importance-of-blank-space-on-your-calendar-c1a5f0e727fc.

Michalowicz, Mike. *Profit First: Transform Your Business from a Cash-Eating Monster to a Money-Making Machine.* Portfolio, 2017.

Qureshi, Asim. "How to Track Time the Elon Musk Way." Jibble, February 19, 2025. https://www.jibble.io/article/track-time-elon-musk-way.

Romaine, Mike. "Serena Williams Workout Routine and Diet Plan: Train like The GOAT of Women's Tennis." Superhero Jacked. Last updated March 10, 2022. https://superherojacked.com/2019/12/19/serena-williams-workout/.

Schwantes, Marcel. "Richard Branson's Best Advice on Hiring the Right People Is a Master Class in Leadership." Inc., April 29, 2014. https://www.inc.com/marcel-schwantes/richard-bransons-best-advice-on-hiring-right-people.html

Silvestre, Dan. "Steve Jobs Insane Productivity Secrets." *The Startup* (blog). Medium, September 7, 2018. https://medium.com/swlh/steve-jobs-insane-productivity-secrets-470e99c482f6.

Stetka, Bret. "Spark Creativity with Thomas Edison's Napping Technique," *Scientific American*, December 9, 2021. https://www.scientificamerican.com/article/thomas-edisons-naps-inspire-a-way-to-spark-your-own-creativity/?

Syverson, Garrett. "Double Your Productivity Overnight with Elon Musk's Time Management Method." Blog. Medium, February 20, 2024. https://medium.com/%40syversonsolution/double-your-productivity-overnight-with-elon-musks-time-management-method-482e1312d845.

Olsen, Susana. "10 Productivity Secrets You Can Learn From Thomas Edison." *The Hours Blog* (blog). Medium, August 20, 2015. https://medium.com/the-hours-blog/10-productivity-secrets-you-can-learn-from-thomas-edison-40e80f3ec10b.

Oprah. "Eight Energy Moves." Accessed February 25, 2025.
https://www.oprah.com/omagazine/solving-the-emotional-energy-crisis_1/all.

Time etc. "6 Time Management Techniques From The World's Most Successful
Business Leaders." Accessed February 24, 2025.
https://www.timeetc.com/resources/how-to-achieve-more/6-time-
management-techniques-from-the-worlds-most-successful-business-leaders?

Von Tobel, Alexa. "How Spanx Founder Sara Blakely Went From Selling Fax
Machines to Shapewear." Inc. June 2, 2023. https://www.inc.com/alexa-von-
tobel/sara-blakely-spanx-founders-project.html?

Ward, Marguerite. "What 9 self-made millionaires do before breakfast." *CNBC*,
September 6, 2016. https://www.cnbc.com/2016/09/06/what-9-self-made-
millionaires-do-before-breakfast.html.

About the Author

Speaker and coach Cindy is the founder of CBC – Cindy Baker Coaching, a coaching and education company for entrepreneurs. With a master's in counseling and over nineteen years as an educator, Cindy's mission is to share the success secrets she has discovered in her own journey as an entrepreneur with ADHD to inspire other creative professionals to leverage their brain's superpowers to become positive, prepared, and productive. Her productivity training has helped countless entrepreneurs grow their businesses by preventing the feeling of being overwhelmed, gaining clarity and focus, and managing their time.

Fueled by faith and coffee, she loves being a wife, grandma, and dog mom. When not speaking or coaching she can be found singing in her church's choir or spending time outdoors.

Having been described by her clients as energetic, positive, a dynamic speaker, caring, and knowledgeable, she is in high demand as a speaker and coach. To find out more about Cindy's courses and coaching programs or to book her as a speaker, you can contact her at cindy@cindybakercoaching.com.

www.ingramcontent.com/pod-product-compliance
Lightning Source LLC
Chambersburg PA
CBHW061708120626
46550CB00003B/1143